Crafts from Papier-Mâché

by Violaine Lamérand

Translated by Cheryl L. Smith

Reading Consultant:
Dr. Robert Miller
Professor of Special Education
Minnesota State University, Mankato

Bridgestone Books
an imprint of Capstone Press
Mankato, Minnesota

Table of contents

words to know

acrylic paint (uh-KRIL-ik PAINT)—a type of paint made from chemicals

corrugated cardboard (KOR-uh-gayt-ed KARD-bord)—cardboard formed with alternating ridges and grooves on the inside

elastic string (ee-LASS-tik STRING)—thin cord that can stretch out and return to its original size and shape

gesso (JEH-so)—a white powder mixed with glue for use in painting; gesso is used to prepare surfaces for paint.

varnish (VAR-nish)—to protect with a thick liquid that dries clear

---

Originally published as *Papier Mâché,* © 1998 Editions Milan.

Bridgestone Books are published by Capstone Press
151 Good Counsel Drive, P.O. Box 669, Mankato, Minnesota 56002
http://www.capstone-press.com

Library of Congress Cataloging-in-Publication Data
Lamérand, Violaine.
    Crafts from papier-mâché/by Violaine Lamérand; translated by
Cheryl L. Smith.
    p. cm.—(Step by step)
    Summary: Provides step-by-step instructions for making twelve
crafts from newspaper, wallpaper paste, paint, and household objects.
    ISBN 0-7368-1478-7 (hardcover)
    1. Papier-mâché—Juvenile literature. [1. Papier-mâché.
2. Handicraft.] I. Title. II. Step by step (Mankato, Minn.)
TT871 .L35 2003
745.54'2—dc21
                                    2002002444

Editor:
Rebecca Glaser

Photographs:
Milan/Dominique Chauvet;
Capstone Press/Gary Sundermeyer

Graphic Design:
Sarbacane

Design Production:
Steve Christensen

1 2 3 4 5 6 07 06 05 04 03 02

Little Secrets about papier-Mâché

To make papier-mâché (PAY-pur-muh-SHAY), you need newspaper and wallpaper paste. Other materials are listed at the beginning of each activity. Read the suggestions carefully and you will succeed in your projects.

2 Prepare the glue by mixing 4 tablespoons (60 mL) of wallpaper paste with ½ cup (125 mL) of water. The paste should be thick, like jelly.

1 Tear the newspaper into strips. Newspaper sometimes tears in straighter strips from one direction. Test a corner first to see which direction works better.

3 Dip your fingers into the wallpaper paste and spread it on the strips of paper. You can also use a paintbrush to apply the paste. Wipe off the extra paste on the side of the bowl. Stick on one strip at a time. Cover the object with seven layers by crisscrossing the strips. Cardboard objects only need three layers to cover them.

VASELINE

 Use masking tape to attach parts before covering them with paper strips.

You can mold objects such as bowls and plates. Cover the objects with Vaseline before covering them with paper strips. The Vaseline makes it easier to remove the papier-mâché from the object when the papier-mâché is dry.

7 Paint your creation with acrylic paint. You can varnish your creation with help from an adult.

6 Let your pieces dry for one or two days. Then paint on a coat of gesso or white acrylic paint to cover the paper strips.

Juggling Balls

2 Add more newspaper around the rock and continue until you have the size of ball you want. Hold the paper with masking tape.

1 Crumple some newspaper around a rock.

3 Cover your ball with glued strips of paper. Make four or five layers. Let it dry well.

8

4 Paint the ball white, then in color. Decorate the ball with patterns of your choice.

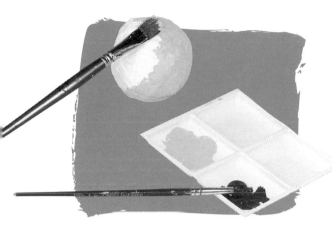

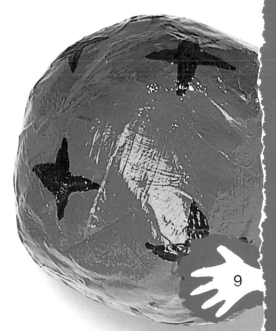

9

 Papier-mâché means chewed paper.

Bowling Pins

You Will Need:
- Small plastic bottles (soda, water, or juice bottles)
- Masking tape
- Paint
- Paintbrush

1 Form a ball of crumpled newspaper around the neck of a bottle. Attach it with masking tape.

2 Cover the bottle with several layers of glued strips, making sure to cover the ball well. Let it dry completely.

3 Paint the object white and then with colors. Create different characters. For a bowling game, make 10 bowling pins Use the balls from page 9.

In the mid-1800s, people in the United States placed bets on bowling games. The state of Connecticut made bowling at nine pins illegal. One story says that people added a tenth pin to get around the law. Tenpin bowling is popular in America today.

Teddy Bear Coat Hanger

You Will Need:

- Coat hanger
- Masking tape
- Cardboard
- Paint
- Paintbrush

1 Make a ball with crumpled newspaper in the center of the coat hanger. Attach it with masking tape.

2 Form a smaller ball with newspaper to make the snout. Cut out two ears from the cardboard. Attach the snout and the ears with masking tape.

3 Cover the head of the bear with several layers of glued newspaper strips. Cover the rest of the coat hanger with newspaper. Let it dry.

4 Paint the hanger white, then with colors.

12

→ The earliest known use of papier-mâché was in China. The Chinese made papier-mâché pot lids and helmets around 220 A.D.

13

strawberry Mask

You Will Need:

- Balloon
- Scissors
- Cotton swab
- Green paper
- Stapler
- Elastic string
- Paint
- Paintbrush

1 Blow up the balloon and cover half of it with seven layers of glued newspaper strips. It is better to put on too many layers than too few. Let it dry well.

3 Paint the mask white, then with color. Dip the cotton swab in paint to make little dots.

2 Pop the balloon. Cut off the edges of the newspaper. Ask an adult to cut out the eyes, mouth, and two holes for the nose.

4 Cut out four leaves from the green paper. Staple them to the top of the mask. Cut a rectangular piece of paper and roll it to make a stem. Staple the stem to hold it. Make four slits on one end, fold them back, and staple the stem to the leaves. To wear your mask, staple elastic string to the inside.

14

Strawberries are a healthy food. They provide vitamin C, which helps your body fight colds.

Necklace and Bracelets

You Will Need:
- Wooden skewer
- Masking tape
- Cotton swabs
- Cord
- Paint
- Paintbrush

1 Roll a strip of glued newspaper around a skewer. Crumple it a bit as you roll to form beads with the paper. Continue to make more beads of different sizes.

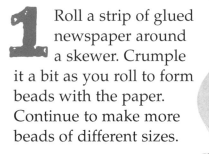

2 Crumple and roll a page of newspaper to make a long, skinny piece. Form it into a ring. Attach the ends with masking tape. Cover it with bands of glued newspaper.

3 When the objects are dry, paint them white. Then paint them with color. Dip a cotton swab in paint to make little dots. When the paint is dry, string the beads on a cord.

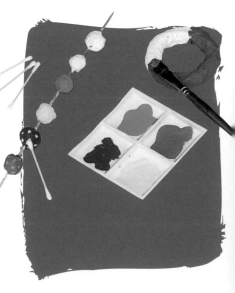

→ Wasps make a natural form of
papier-mâché. Female wasps chew
up plant fibers or old wood to make
paper for their nests.

17

Plates and Bowls

You Will Need:

- Plate and bowl
- Vaseline
- Scissors
- Eraser or potato
- Paint
- Paintbrush

1 Smear the plate and the bowl with Vaseline. Then cover it with seven crisscrossed layers of papier-mâché.

2 When the newspaper is completely dry, remove the plate and bowl. Cut off the rough edges. Fold short strips of paper and crisscross them over the edge. Let them dry.

3 Paint the dishes white. Then paint in color.

4 Ask an adult to cut the eraser or potato into a triangle shape for stamping. Dip the end in paint and stamp triangles around the edge of your dish. When the paint is dry, you can varnish the dishes.

Use these dishes as decorations or to
hold small items like keys and coins.

ornaments

You Will Need:

- Corrugated cardboard
- Scissors
- Paper clips
- Masking tape
- Ribbon
- Paint
- Paintbrush

2 Cover the cardboard with two or three layers of glued newspaper strips. Let them dry.

3 Paint the shapes white, then with color. When they are dry, tie colored ribbons to the paper clips.

1 Cut out shapes from the cardboard. Tape a paper clip on the back side with masking tape. Let it stick out a bit.

You can hang these ornaments in your room as decorations.

21

Pencil Holder

2 Cover the outside with at least three layers of glued newspaper strips. Cover the inside with one layer. Let it dry.

3 Paint the inside and the outside with white paint, then with color. Let the paint dry. Then cut out shapes from the colored paper and glue them on to make windows and doors.

1 Cut out the cartons so each is a different height. Join them together with masking tape.

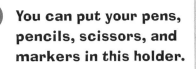

You can put your pens,
pencils, scissors, and
markers in this holder.

23

PuppetS

2 Form balls of newspaper to make the hair and nose. Dip the balls in the glue and stick them to the head. Attach them with short strips of glued paper. Cover the rest of the head with strips of glued paper. Let it dry.

3 Paint with white, then in color. Put a sock around the neck. Cut off the bottom and make two holes for your fingers. Your index finger goes into the head of your puppet.

1 Ask an adult to help you cut off the top of the bottle. On the neck of the bottle, attach a ball of crumpled newspaper with masking tape for the head.

24

A hobo clown cannot play a trick on a whiteface clown. But a whiteface clown can play tricks on anybody.

Maracas

You Will Need:
- **2 small balloons (as for water balloons)**
- **Dried beans, noodles, or sand**
- **2 cardboard tubes**
- **Masking tape**
- **Paint**
- **Paintbrush**

1 Blow up a balloon and tie a knot. Cover it with seven layers of papier-mâché. Do not cover the knot. Let the papier-mâché dry completely.

2 Hold the knot with one hand and burst the balloon. Pull out the balloon and pour some dried beans, noodles, or sand into the shape. Close the hole with a few strips of papier-mâché. Let it dry.

3 Attach the cardboard tube with masking tape.

4 Cover the tube with several layers of glued paper strips. Let it dry.

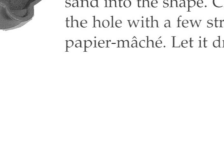

Shake your maracas to the beat of your favorite music. Try putting different materials in your maracas. Large beans will make a heavy sound. Sand will make a lighter sound.

5 Paint with white, then with color.

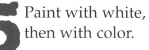

Snowman Bank

You Will Need:
- 2 small balloons
- Masking tape
- Cardboard
- Scissors
- Small yogurt cup
- 2 small sticks
- Paint
- Paintbrush
- Glue

1 Blow up a balloon and tie a knot. Blow up another balloon, but make it a little smaller. Join the balloons with masking tape. Cut feet out of the cardboard.

2 Cover both balloons with seven layers of papier-mâché. Add a few strips to make the scarf. Make a carrot shape with newspaper for the nose. Attach it with glued strips of newspaper. Cover the feet with three layers of papier-mâché.

3 When the snowman is dry, ask an adult to cut out the mouth and a circle the size of the yogurt cup on top of the head. Pop the balloons. Then paint the snowman.

28

4 Glue the feet under the body and glue the sticks to the sides. Fill the yogurt cup with a rolled up strip of cardboard. Paint the hat. It will be the stopper to your bank.

How many pennies can you collect for your bank? Did you know that pennies were made from steel instead of copper during World War II (1939-1945)? Copper was hard to find during the war.

29

Dog

You Will Need:

- 1 short cardboard tube
- 1 long cardboard tube
- Masking tape
- Corrugated cardboard
- Thin cardboard
- Scissors

1 Attach the two tubes at an angle with masking tape to make the neck and body. Cut two ears from the corrugated cardboard.

2 Cover the body with crumpled newspaper. Form a long head and attach it to the neck. Attach the ears with masking tape.

3 Cut four pieces from the thin cardboard. Roll them and tape them closed. Make four slits in one end and fold them outward. Attach the tubes to the body to make legs. Make a tail out of the thin cardboard. Cut slits in the end and fold them out to attach the tail to the body.

4 Cover the dog with several layers of papier-mâché. Make sure you cover the feet well. Let it dry.

→ Dogs have a good sense of smell. They can sniff out illegal drugs and follow trails of people who are lost.

5 Paint with white, then with color.

31

Index

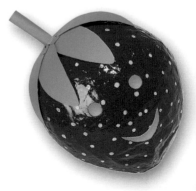